Missy Herre
You. Love
your labor of love. Be
encouraged.
2/12/23

Love you!
Lady Wooten

GOD Against COVID-19

GOD AGAINST COVID-19

By
International Evangelist Lady
Shirley A. Wooten

XULON PRESS

Xulon Press
2301 Lucien Way #415
Maitland, FL 32751
407.339.4217
www.xulonpress.com

© 2022 by International Evangelist Lady Shirley A. Wooten

All rights reserved solely by the author. The author guarantees all contents are original and do not infringe upon the legal rights of any other person or work. No part of this book may be reproduced in any form without the permission of the author.

Due to the changing nature of the Internet, if there are any web addresses, links, or URLs included in this manuscript, these may have been altered and may no longer be accessible. The views and opinions shared in this book belong solely to the author and do not necessarily reflect those of the publisher. The publisher therefore disclaims responsibility for the views or opinions expressed within the work.

Unless otherwise indicated, Scripture quotations taken from the King James Version (KJV) – *public domain.*

Paperback ISBN-13: 978-1-6628-5635-8
Ebook ISBN-13: 978-1-6628-5636-5

This book is dedicated to my wonderful husband, Bishop Lawrence M. Wooten, Pastor of Williams Temple COGIC, Second Assistant Presiding Bishop, Church of God In Christ, who has been there for me through every test and trial. It is also dedicated to my dear mother, Mrs. Hattie Adkins, deceased at 94 years old and who instilled Christian values in me as a child. This book is also dedicated to my dear father, Mr. Hugh Adkins, who went home to be with the Lord on October 3, 1991.

Thanks to Tena Anderson for typing and proofreading, Dr. Lillie Faison and Dr. Evelyn Carter for proofreading, and Dr. Peggie Smith for her support.

CONTENTS

Foreword xi
Introduction xiii

Chapter 1   All-Powerful God 1
Chapter 2   The Demon COVID-19 7
Chapter 3   COVID-19 Attack Against
                Bishop L. M. Wooten and Family 11
Chapter 4   COVID-19 Attack Against Mother
                Hattie Adkins 17
Chapter 5   Ten Steps to Victory over COVID-19
                or Any Other Problem 25
Chapter 6   Deliverance in Your Praise 31
Chapter 7   Just a Test 35
Chapter 8   Contend for the Faith 41
Chapter 9   40 Day Worldwide Fast and Prayer 47
Chapter 10 Summary 59

Warfare Prayer 61
Family Photo Gallery 62
Biography 69
Bibliography 73

FOREWORD

My sister, International Evangelist Shirley A. Wooten, is a lady of prayer, confidence, determination, and righteousness. My childhood memories of my sister's determination were exemplified through her hard work on the farm while in Southampton County, yet making excellent grades in all subjects. After high school, Virginia State University was her choice for higher education where she majored in English education and excelled there while tutoring others and serving others with the Alpha Kappa Alpha Sorority.

She later studied at Syracuse University in Public Relations, and her gift of writing took her to various cities. Her last stop was St. Louis, Missouri. She worked as a Writer Producer for various companies in Syracuse, New Jersey and St. Louis. While in Missouri, she heard God's call to serve others through prayer, the word, and giving. God led her to bring "the Glory Train": a flatbed 18-wheeler truck with singers, snacks, and preachers, to calm the streets during the riots in Ferguson Missouri. From the streets and across the globe, Evangelist Shirley A. Wooten has followed the instructions of God.

While there are several books on healing and triumph, few of them have been designed to meet the needs of those who are seeking to heal from the "invisible enemy," COVID-19.

Evangelist Shirley Adkins Wooten has courageously accepted the challenge of engaging the reader on how God can lead the way in surviving the coronavirus.

This book will guide the reader through events involving our family and COVID-19, and how God guided Evangelist Shirley through His words and verses from the Bible.

Pastors, Christian educators, students, and Christians will discover that my sister's book can become a tool for instruction, reference, and inspiration.

In *God Against Covid,* Evangelist Shirley A. Wooten gives you the roadmap of how God worked with her to battle COVID-19, which has ravaged 182 countries, but Evangelist Shirley saw the hand of God move.

Dr. Evelyn Adkins Carter
EAC Consulting, LLC

INTRODUCTION

You are about to witness a powerful testimony of how the almighty God triumphed over the dreadful, deadly COVID-19 virus in the life of the Wooten and Adkins family. The devil thought he had us, but we got away! Many died of the virus, but God delivered us in the midst of the pandemic, out of the fiery furnace, without the smell of smoke.

Isaiah 54:17 says, "No weapon formed against you shall prosper and every tongue which rises against you in judgment you shall condemn. This is the heritage of the servants of the Lord, and their righteousness is from Me says the Lord;" the weapon formed against our family, but it *did not prosper!*

You must understand that God is almighty and all-powerful, and there is nothing too hard for God. If you have faith the size of a mustard seed, God will move mountains in your life. But you will have to really *see* it by faith before you can *see it!*

God always prepares His people for treacherous storms headed their way. "Many are the afflictions of the righteous but the Lord delivers him out of them all" (Psalm 34:19). In November 2019, God appeared to me in a series of dreams. He said that something terrible was about to happen in our midst. A great shaking was going to take place, and we needed to be ready. And it came to pass, with COVID-19.

God always leads, guides, and directs His people in unusual ways. God instructed us to call an anointed citywide forty-day fast and shut-in from December 2, 2019, to January 10, 2020, to cry out against crime in St. Louis. People from throughout the nation and Africa joined in the fast and shut-in. My husband, General Board Member Bishop Lawrence Wooten, and I ate no food for forty days, and I was shut-in in the sanctuary all forty days, and God blessed. Many souls were saved, blessed, and delivered during the shut-in.

We were praying against crime, but God was also preparing us for the vicious COVID-19 attack coming against our nation and family. In Psalm 139:4, we read, "Even before there is a word on my tongue, behold, O Lord, you know it all." There is good in every trial. For Romans 8:28 says, "And we know that all things work together for good to those who love God, as those who are the called according to His purpose." God works behind the scenes. Whatever happens in your life is working for your good. You may not see it now, but hold on, and it will be revealed at the appointed time.

So, in the midst of our COVID-19 dilemma, we knew that God would bring us out with the victory with a mighty outstretched hand. God is all-powerful and almighty, and there is nothing too hard for our God.

C Christ
O Offers
V Victory
I in
D Disease

Chapter 1

All-Powerful God

Before we talk about COVID-19, let's talk about the power of God. God is all- powerful, and there is nothing too hard for my God. It was God who created the heavens and the earth in the beginning by the power of His spoken word. Genesis 1:3 says, "And God said let there be light and there was light." "And God went on to say, "Let there be a firmament"... in the midst of the waters...let the water under the heaven be gathered together...let the earth bring forth grass...let there be lights in the firmament," ... And it came to pass through God's spoken word.

God is a God of miracles. If you can believe it, He will perform it. We really need to remove the word *impossible* from our vocabulary. We give satan too much power and authority. He only has the power of deception through FEAR: False Evidence Appearing Real. So, we need to rebuke the evil devil and cast him out of our minds and put him where he belongs—under our feet, in Jesus' name.

We must hold on to the promises of God by faith. Hebrews 11:1 says, "Now faith is the substance of things hoped for and the evidence of things not seen." To fight COVID-19 and any other affliction, we must fight the good fight of faith and hold on to God's unchanging hand. Get a bulldog's hold and don't let go. God sees your faith through your actions. So, rebuke the spirit of doubt and unbelief.

God is not moved by tears and sweat. Only mountain-moving mustard-seed faith moves God. So then faith comes by hearing and hearing by the Word of God. Your faith increases when you hear yourself say the Word. So, say "I am healed", say "I am delivered," "I am prosperous," "I am blessed." Your faith activates the power of God in your situation.

Power signifies authority and dominion, and the Godhead has total authority over everything. God's strength and authority are limitless. He is all-powerful. The term we usually hear describing the idea of God being all-powerful is *omnipotence*, which is a Latin word that means "all power." God has all power in His hand. Trust Him, believe Him, and receive His promises.

When you go to the store, you give the cashier money in exchange for goods. You go to God and give Him your faith in exchange for what you want or need. God will give you the desires of your heart—*only believe!*

We see God's great power in Exodus when God delivered His people from bondage in Egypt. Along with creation, this is the one event that the Israelites always referred back to remind each other of the power of God. God also referred to this event many times to remind His people of His power. God has all power.

Deuteronomy 4:37 states, "Because He loved your fathers, therefore He chose their descendants after them. And He personally bought you from Egypt by His great power. But the Lord who brought you up from the land of Egypt with great power and with an outstretched arm, Him you shall fear, and to Him you shall bring yourself down and to Him you shall sacrifice".

All the plagues showed God's power over nature and over the so-called gods of the Egyptians. We know that God completed the deliverance of His people by showing His power in parting the Red Sea, so His people could walk through on dry ground. I see you walking through the floods and fire! In Exodus 14:30 Moses wrote, "Thus, the Lord saved Israel that day from the hand of the Egyptians and Israel saw the Egyptians dead on the seashore. And when Israel saw the great power which the Lord had used against the Egyptians the people feared the Lord, and they believed in the Lord and in His servant Moses"

God's power was also displayed in providing daily sustenance to His people in the wilderness. He gave them manna on a daily basis. He provided water. He gave them quail to eat. He gives to all men everything they need for life. We also see Jesus' power so clearly within the gospel accounts. There are so many miracles that show that He is God and has all power!

God has power *over diseases*. He healed the lame, healed those with leprosy, made the blind see, made the deaf hear, and made the mute speak. God has power *over nature*. He calmed the raging storm, walked on water, multiplied the fish and the loaves, and filled nets with fish more than once. God has power *over the spiritual realm*. He forgave sins, cast out demons, and raised the dead. You can see in all these things that Jesus did that there is not anything that God cannot do. And He can deliver from COVID-19.

One of my favorite displays of God's power in Scripture is the resurrection of Christ: "His son, who was born of a descendent of David according to the flesh, who was declared the Son of God with power by the resurrection from the dead, according to the Spirit of holiness, Jesus Christ our Lord" (Romans 1:3–4). "In accordance with the working of the strength of His might which he brought about in Christ, God raised Him from the dead and seated Him at His right hand in heavenly places" (Ephesians 1:19–20).

God raised Christ from the dead. Death could not keep Him. Sin and death were defeated with the resurrection. This display of God's strength and power is what gives us the hope that we have. This display of God's power is crucial to our faith.

God has power to forgive and to give salvation to sinners. How does He do this? He does it through the gospel of Jesus Christ. Everything in God's nature has a tie to the glorious gospel of Christ.

"For I am not ashamed of the gospel of Christ: for it is the power of God unto salvation to everyone that believes" (Romans 1:16). The preaching of the gospel is God's power and strength that He uses to deliver the lost people away from the enemy and to make them members of Christ's church. The gospel, and the gospel alone, does this.

This power of God that raised Christ from His tomb can do the same for us. It can raise us out of any sin and other sickness and disease.

His power will resurrect us on the last day. The voice that created the universe will call us out of our tombs of COVID-19 and other afflictions. God will protect us and sustain us. God has power over COVID-19.

"Blessed be the God and Father of our Lord Jesus Christ, who according to His great mercy has caused us to be born again to a living hope through the resurrection of Jesus Christ from the dead, to obtain an inheritance which is imperishable and undefiled and will not fade away, reserved in heaven for you, who are protected by the *power of God* through faith for a salvation ready to be revealed in the last time" (I Peter 1:3).

Our faith must not rest in ourselves and our strength. If that is the case, we will not have much hope. Our faith must rest solely on the power of God to save us from our sin and deliver us from the evil in this world and to bring us to our home in heaven. We cannot do any of these things in our own strength and power. The power of God's Word is sufficient in times of distress. But he said to me, "My grace is sufficient for you, for my power is made perfect in weakness. Therefore, I will boast all the more gladly of my weaknesses, so that the power of Christ may rest upon me. For the sake of Christ, then, I am content with weaknesses, insults, hardships, persecutions, and calamities. For when I am weak, then I am strong" (Corinthians 12:9–10).

Paul prayed three times for God to remove something difficult in his life—a thorn in his flesh. When we pray for our needs, we long to hear from God. During COVID-19, we have a new perspective on our needs. Fear can run rampant as we face a new reality. We seek strength, healing, and God's power in the midst of a global pandemic.

Spending time in God's word gives us the truth that sets us free. We can trust Him with our fears and weaknesses. He reminds us that He's our sufficiency, "enough" for our need. These words are a declaration and promise to strengthen our souls with the faith we need to persevere through pain, panic, and problems. There is nothing too hard for God.

Renew your faith and your strength by looking at the many miracles wrought by God throughout the Bible.

—Jesus changed water to wine (John 2:1–11).
—Jesus cured the nobleman's son (John 4:46–47).
—Jesus made a great haul of fishes (Luke 5:1–11).
—Jesus cast out unclean spirits (Mark 1:23–28).

—Jesus cured Peter's mother-in-law (Mark 1:30–31).
—Jesus healed a leper (Mark 1:40–45).
—Jesus healed a centurion's son (Matt. 8:5–13).
—Jesus raised a widow's son from the dead (Luke 7:11–18).
—Jesus stilled the storm (Matt. 8:23–27).
—Jesus cured a paralytic (Matt. 9:1–8).
—Jesus raised a ruler's daughter from the dead (Matt. 9:18–26).
—Jesus cured a woman with an issue of blood (Luke 8:43–48).
—Jesus opened blinded eyes (Matt. 9:27–31).
—Jesus loosened the tongue of the dumb (Matt. 9:32–33).
—Jesus healed an invalid man at the pool of Bethesda (John 5:1–9).
—Jesus restored a withered hand (Matt. 12:10–13).
—Jesus cured a demon-possessed man (Matt. 12:22).
—Jesus fed at least five thousand people or more (Matt. 14:15–21).
—Jesus healed a woman of Canaan (Matt. 15:22–28).
—Jesus cured a deaf-mute (Mark 7:31–37).
—Jesus fed at least four thousand (Matt. 15:32–39).
—Jesus opened the eyes of a blind man (Mark 8:22–26).
—Jesus cured a boy plagued by a demon (Matt. 17:14–21).
—Jesus opened the eyes of a man born blind (John 9:1–38).
—Jesus cured a woman afflicted for eighteen years (Luke 13:10–17).
—Jesus cured a man of leprosy (Luke 14:1–4).
—Jesus cleansed ten lepers (Luke 17:11–19).
—Jesus raised Lazarus (John 11:1–46).
—Jesus opened the eyes of two blind men (Matt. 20:30–34).
—Jesus caused a fig tree to wither (Matt. 21:18–22).
—Jesus restored the ear of the high priest's servant (Luke 22:50–51).
—Jesus rose from the dead (Luke 24:5–6).

Chapter 2

The Demon COVID-19

Let's examine COVID-19, a demonic spirit. Coronavirus disease 2019 (COVID-19) is a respiratory disease, demonic in nature, that was identified in Wuhan, China, and is now being spread throughout the world. COVID-19 has changed our lives, cancelled sports tournaments, forced school and church closures, and emptied shelves at stores; and fear is rampant. *But God!*

COVID-19 is a demon straight from the pits of hell. It is spread through the air by coughing or sneezing through close personal contact (including touch and shaking hands), or through touching your nose, mouth, or eyes before washing your hands. Symptoms of COVID-19 are fever, cough, shortness of breath, chills, headache, sore throat, loss of taste or smell, and muscle pain. Symptoms may appear from two to fourteen days after exposure. Symptoms can range from mild or no symptoms to severe illness.

There previously was no vaccine to guarantee full protection against COVID-19. The best way to protect yourself is to stay home as much as possible and avoid close contact with others. You should wear a mask that covers your nose and mouth in public settings and practice distancing of six feet, washing hands often with soap and water for at least twenty seconds, and using sanitizer.

American life has been fundamentally reordered because of the virus. Concerts, parades, and games have been cancelled. Unemployment claims have spiked. In some states that reopened early, case levels have surged anew. Churches, and schools have gone from in-person to virtual.

Many have been affected by the delta and omicron variants. There are subtle differences between the variants. All indications suggest omicron is milder than delta and less severe (US Center for Disease Control and Prevention). Omicron patients had a 53% reduced risk of hospitalization. Nevertheless, we have power to rebuke all variants of this disease and pull down strongholds and cast the devil out. Called by any name, God has power over corona!

When facing the fear of the unknown, turning to a powerful, all-knowing God is a good start to responding with clarity and direction. Churches where hugs and handshakes are frequent have transitioned to fist and elbow bumps, which is wise. Writing to the church at Philippi, where he had been beaten and imprisoned, Paul tells the believers, in the book of Philippians, not to worry or to be anxious about anything. Paul instructs them to pray for God's blessings to make supplication for his protection, and to do it all with thanksgiving.

Studies show that prayer reduces anxiety and depression. A reduction in anxiety allows people to process and react to external events in a more cognitive rather than emotional manner. In a time in which there is worldwide concern over a virus with scientists, some politicians, a strategic and peaceful approach to problem solving is a good thing.

Thankfully, God gives believers a resource to stand firm in the face of fear. God has given us Holy Ghost power. Second Timothy 1:7 tells us, "God hath not given us the spirit of fear; but power, and of love, and of a sound mind." The Holy Spirit is a spirit of power. In the context of 2 Timothy 1:8, this power enabled Paul to endure incredible suffering. Notice the next verse: "The Lord grant unto him that he may find mercy of the Lord in that day; and in how many things he ministered unto me at Ephesus, thou knowest very well."

The best news in the world is that we have the Holy Spirit, the promises and seal of the new covenant; and He is a spirit of faith and not a spirit of fear. Jesus died on the cross that COVID-19 might not overtake our faith. Jesus rose again that the power of His resurrection would dwell in us. Jesus came that we might not fear the curses of this world. He broke the curse of sin and death in His body and rose again from the dead to declare them powerless.

Whenever we feel overwhelmed by this chaos, COVID-19, and the difficulty of life, we can turn to God in fervent prayer for peace and serenity. In a time of uncertainty, fear, seclusion, and preparation from what we term "normal," our human solution is to handle it ourselves. But turning to God should be our first response, not our last response. Philippians 4:6 tells us, "Be careful for nothing; but in everything by prayer and supplication with thanksgiving let your requests be made known unto God." "For I reckon that the sufferings of this present time are not worthy to be with the glory which shall be revealed in us." (Romans 8:18).

The truth is, bad things happen to those Jesus loves. Audrey Wetherell Johnson, Author of <u>Created For Commitment</u>, was born in England and educated in Europe. She was an agnostic but transformed by God's grace into a gifted Bible teacher. In the 1930s, she felt God calling her to be a missionary.

After years of teaching in a seminary in a foreign country, Johnson was captured with other missionaries and placed in a concentration camp for three years of unimaginable suffering. When Johnson was finally released, she came to America and began Bible Study Fellowship, an international ministry influencing millions of people of faith to study God's Word each week.

During this very difficult time, we are all going to suffer in one way or another. I pray that it is in a minor way. Lean on Jesus for your strength, and keep your faith strong. When something bad happens to you, look forward to the glory that is coming.

Chapter 3

COVID-19 Attack Against Bishop L. M. Wooten and Family

When news of COVID-19 was publicized, we immediately began to educate ourselves on the virus. At Williams Temple Church in the Eastern Missouri Western Illinois Jurisdiction, on March 8, 2020, for Sunday morning services, we scheduled Dr. Eric Kondro, medical doctor, and Loretta Rodgers, registered nurse, to conduct a forty- minute training session with the congregation on how to avoid contracting COVID-19. It was very informative, followed by a question-and-answer session with detailed handout materials.

Our Eastern Missouri Western Illinois Jurisdiction workers' meeting was held from March 11 to 13, 2020. On March 11, we had a brief session to educate the jurisdiction on COVID-19, instructing them to avoid handshaking, hugging, close contact, etc. As a family, we followed all guidelines that we knew of at that time to prevent contracting the virus.

We found out later that the virus broke out in many COGIC jurisdictions throughout the nation at the workers' meetings, and many saints died during this time. God blessed through our workers' meeting with no virus outbreaks. Praise God!

During the week of March 16, 2020, Bishop Wooten and our daughter Grace went to the bank to exchange coins and to Office Depot. None of the rest of the family had left the house to go to any stores, etc. in over a month. Our family at home consists of me, Shirley Wooten, 72; Bishop Wooten, 82; Grace, 17; Sarah, 16; and housekeeper Kim Small, 55. We are all saved and Holy Ghost–filled. After having gone out the week of March 16, 2020, Grace became very sick with what we thought was the flu. She had severe vomiting, diarrhea, high temperature, coughing, fatigue, and nosebleeds. She did not tell us at the time, but we found out from Sarah later that she had difficulty breathing. She also had no appetite. I isolated her somewhat, but she and Bishop did the census together at the computer. I gave her Mucinex and liquids, and after about two weeks, she was well. It did not cross my mind at that time that she may have had COVID-19. Now, I believe, she had the virus and perhaps got it at the bank with the coin machine.

My husband, Bishop Wooten, had begun to cough some and had a red eye, but no other symptoms. On March 27, 2020, we were casually sitting at the table. Bishop Wooten had just finished eating breakfast. Suddenly, he had a convulsion and began to violently shake and vomit. Then he slumped over unconscious, no pulse, with eyes and mouth opened…. dead. Then all his bodily fluids broke loose, including his bowels, and I knew he was dead. I knew this was a sign of death, but I told death not so—not today!

How dare death sneak up in my house to steal my husband! Matthew 11:12 tells us "And from the days of John the Baptist until now the Kingdom of heaven suffereth violence, and the violent take it by force." I grabbed his head and began to rebuke death, and commanded him to live and not die. I prayed over him in the Holy Ghost, and took authority over Satan and snatched him from death's door.

I was so loud everyone in the house came running. Sarah, startled, said he looked dead. I told her to get a cold towel, and she ran and told Kim to call 911 and told Grace to get ice. Suddenly, he began to breathe and cough at a fast pace as life came back into his limp body, after I travailed in prayer about 5 minutes. Bishop Wooten did not recall what happened. He said he felt weak, and he was headed towards bright lights, which we know was heaven. To be absent from the body is to be present with the Lord. He had experienced death and going to heaven.

James 5:16 says, "Confess your faults one to another, and pray one for another, that ye may be healed. The effectual fervent prayer of a righteous man availeth much." His eyes slowly opened, and I knew death was defeated in Jesus' name.

The ambulance arrived, and the paramedics said his blood pressure was okay and heart seemed okay. They said the emergency room was packed with COVID-19 patients and did not recommend taking him there due to his age. So we cleaned him up and put him to bed. I called his doctor, who said if this happened again, we should take him to the hospital. The weapon was formed, but I knew it would not prosper, according to Isaiah 54:17, which says "No weapon that is formed against thee shall prosper, and every tongue that shall rise against thee in judgment thou shalt condemn. This is the heritage of the servants of the Lord, and their righteousness is of me saith the Lord." The devil was defeated and God was exalted.

That night he was fine, only weak. The next day, March 28, we were sitting at the table. I told the kids, "Let's go for a walk and exercise." We got dressed and went to the door. Suddenly, it started to rain. I went back and sat at the table with Bishop and told him it was raining, so we were not going to walk. As I sat down, suddenly, his head dropped, and he went into a violent seizure and then went unconscious again. His eyes and mouth again had the look of death, no pulse, I knew death had returned. Again, I grabbed his head and began to rebuke death. I went into violent spiritual warfare, praying for his life, binding death. I stood on Matthew 18:18, which says, "Verily I say unto you, Whatsoever ye shall bind on earth shall be bound in heaven; and whatsoever ye shall loose on earth shall be loosed in heaven."

The whole family again came running when they heard me praying. Thank God for the rain! It saved his life. Psalm 37:23 tells, "The steps of a good man are ordered by the Lord: and he delighteth in his way." After about five minutes, he came back to life, coughing. I believe, he died again. We called the ambulance, but I drove him to Barnes West County Hospital because ambulances could not transport the distance. At the emergency room, after I told them what had happened the past two days, they immediately tested him for COVID-19. Bishop Wooten did not recall having the seizures, etc. He only recalled being tired. He remembered going up and seeing bright lights – going to heaven. Praise God! I am so glad he came back twice! His work was not done on earth.

Bishop Wooten's doctor, Dr. Zamir Eidleman, told him that he was a miracle to be alive because of his age. Death came for him twice, but God said no! He was quarantined for 34 days. The virus was new, and I wanted to be cautious. During his thirty-four days of quarantine, he called into the church prayer line daily and prayed, preached virtual at 11 a.m. on Sunday and most Tuesdays on Facebook live, and participated in various Zoom meetings. No one knew he was in quarantine in his room. He gave no place to the devil. He was stronger than ever and had a good appetite. He stood on Nehemiah 8:10, which says, "Then he said unto them, Go your way, eat the fat, and drink the sweet, and send portions unto them for whom nothing is prepared: for this day is holy unto our Lord: neither be ye sorry; for the joy of the Lord is your strength." The prayer of the righteous casted out all symptoms of COVID-19!

You cannot tell people everything because people will put you in the grave before your time. On April 30, Bishop Wooten came out of quarantine, doing great and told the saints his testimony. They rejoiced! We both were tested to see if we had the antibodies against the virus, and we both had antibodies, according to scientists, because I had the antibodies, at some point, I had COVID-19 without any illness or symptoms. Praise God! Jeremiah 32:27 tells me, "Behold, I am the Lord, the God of all flesh; is there anything too hard for me?"

God is a miracle worker, and He can do the impossible. Matthew 17:20 says, "And Jesus said unto them, Because of your unbelief: for verily I say unto you, If ye have faith as a grain of mustard seed, ye shall say unto this mountain, Remove hence to yonder place; and it shall remove; and nothing shall be impossible unto you."

The mountain had to move out of our way. Many in the COGIC and throughout the world died of COVID-19, but God was merciful toward us and spared our lives. Our God is greater than COVID-19, if we believe it. Thank You, Jesus! We give Him praise and glory for His marvelous acts. We are so grateful to God for sparing Grace's life, Bishop's life, and my life and our entire household. Our entire family has tested negative for

COVID-19. Glory to God! We could have lost another COGIC General Board Member and his wife and daughter, but God said, "no". "But thanks be to God who giveth us the victory through our Lord Jesus Christ" (1 Corinthians 15:57).

CHAPTER 4

COVID-19 Attack Against Mother Hattie Adkins

The COVID-19 demon also attacked my ninety-three-year-old mother, Mrs. Hattie Adkins, weighing just seventy-nine pounds, at the nursing home in Alexandria, Virginia. She had no other major health issues. Praise God! We were informed that a patient and an employee at the nursing home had the virus. We decided to remove my Mom from the nursing home, not knowing that she had already contracted it. We were told that she had not had any contact with those infected and she did not have COVID-19. We asked the nursing home to test her before we removed her, but they refused, which was a big mistake on their part. We took her out of the nursing home on April 30, 2019, and took her to be tested the same day. We did not get the positive test results until May 7, 2020, through a letter in the mail. At that point, she had been amongst family members and had been placed in a house with several twenty-four-hour around-the-clock health-care workers.

When we found out Mom had COVID, immediately the home health-care workers and family went into quarantine and went to be tested for the virus. Praise God, everyone tested negative. John 15:7 says, "If ye abide in me, and my words abide in you, ye shall ask what ye will, and it shall be done unto you." Everyone quit the job, and now there was no one to care for Mom, who had COVID-19. My sisters had other situations and could not keep her. I was the only one who could come and care for Mom until she tested negative or other arrangements were made. I was willing to risk my life for my Mom. My sisters Lillie, Peggie, and Evelyn were very supportive, along with Latorial, Michelle, Carl, and Covington. I could not have made it without them.

I flew to Norfolk, Virginia, from St. Louis, Missouri, on May 8 to live with and care for my Mom in Boykins, Virginia. I knew that I could contract the virus and die, but I put my total trust and confidence in God, believing that He would protect me, as he had done when Bishop had the virus. There were no other options, and my dear husband, Bishop Wooten, agreed to allow me to go. I stood on Psalm 31:1 which says, "In thee, O Lord, do I put my trust; let me never be ashamed: deliver me in thy righteousness," and Psalm 71:1, "In thee, O Lord, do I put my trust: let me never be put to confusion." My St. Louis friends were all worried about me, but I knew God was in control.

Mom was located in a house next door to my sister Lillie, in the Boykins Neighborhood Outreach Center. In the six-room center, they had set up a very lovely handicapped room just for Mom, with a big-screen TV, flowers, handicapped bed, and all necessities. This house is owned by my sister, where she mentors neighborhood children. It was closed due to the virus and had become the Boykins Rehab Center, according to Mom.

The saints throughout the US and friends in Africa were praying for Mom's deliverance and my protection. Mom had no symptoms other than severe coughing. This was a miracle in itself at ninety-three years old, with a low immune system and little appetite and few symptoms. (Psalm 91:15) states, "He shall call upon me, and I will answer him: I will be with him in trouble; I will deliver him, and honour him."

When I arrived in Virginia, Mom was totally bedridden. She was very thin, weighing only seventy-nine pounds at five feet four. She could not sit herself up or get up alone. My job was to bathe and dress her, feed her, change her, give medications, and totally take care of her. She was like a baby, and I was responsible for twenty-four-hour care alone. She did not want to eat or get out of the bed.

Through days of prayer, fasting, and the cries of the righteous, she began to eat more. God gave her strength to sit herself up, get up, and eventually walk with her walker and go to the pot with assistance. I used every trick in the book to get her to eat. I even paid her to eat. She liked money. We even had a song called "Eat and Fight the Virus," which I sang to get her to eat.

I even spoon-fed her at times. She suffered from some Alzheimer's and dementia and did not like to eat. She needed nutrition to build up her immune system to fight COVID-19.

She would not wear a mask because she would spit and cough all day. I had my gloves and mask but no shield in the beginning. Later I got goggles and a shield from my sisters. I also started to wear a robe and change often. I washed my hands frequently and used sanitizer. I slept in a different room but used the same air-conditioning system. My fate was in God's hands. She had no major symptoms, but I was told she could pass the virus, and someone else would have all the symptoms and die. I stood on the Word and did what I knew to protect myself. Jeremiah 26:14 says, "As for me, behold, I am in your hand: do with me as seemeth good and meet unto you."

On May 18, I convinced the county health department to come to the house to test Mom and me again. After much pleading, they agreed. God gave favor. To my surprise, on May 20, we got the results that we *both* tested positive with the virus, but I had no symptoms as before when I caught it from Bishop. Acts 28:3 states, "And when Paul had gathered a bundle of sticks, and laid them on the fire, there came a viper out of the heat, and fastened on his hand." With the snake latched on to Paul's hand, he shook him off and had no harm. I shook the virus off and had no symptoms or harm. Praise God! But my first thought from satan, was, "My God, my God, why hast thou forsaken me?" My sister Dr. Lillie Faison reminded me, "You are not forsaken; you have no symptoms. You are yet strong and healthy." I said, "You are right!" The weapon formed against me, but it did not prosper. I shook the devil off!

Mom was so sad that I had caught the virus. I told her, "Don't be sad, because it will go away." She tried to come up with other ways I could have gotten it. She said I got the virus…

1) On a cruise a year ago
2) From a trip to Africa years ago
3) Maybe I had contact with the man from China who brought it to the US
4) Maybe on the plane

I said, "Mom, don't worry about it. We will get over it and be fine."

She was so funny coming up with how I got the virus, but quite serious.

I started taking various vitamins, supplements, and teas recommended by my sister Dr. Peggie Smith to fight the virus: vitamin D, vitamin C, zinc, elderberry zinc lozenges, ginger chews, lemon ginger tea, turmeric ginger tea, echinacea plus tea, elderberry syrup, and Vicks VapoRub. All of these remedies were very helpful, and I was in good shape, physically, with no symptoms.

I also tried without much success to encourage Mom to take the supplements. She said that if the doctor didn't prescribe it, she didn't want it.

Also, before coming to Virginia, I had walked two miles five days a week, either outside or with the Walk Away the Pounds tape by Leslie Sansone. So I was in good physical shape, which is essential to fighting disease.

Most importantly, I continued in prayer and travail, and I felt the prayers of the righteous. I stood on James 5:16 that says, "Confess your faults one to another; and pray one for another, that ye may be healed. The effectual fervent prayer of a righteous man availeth much," and Matthew 7:7 which says, "Ask, and it shall be given you; seek, and ye shall find; knock, and it shall be opened unto you:"

Our plan was after Mom tested negative; we would hire another staff of health- care workers to care for her. But I began to realize that she needed twenty-four-hour care at the long-term facility. Mom had a bell. She would ring it or call for me at 1 a.m., 3 a.m., 5 a.m., 7 a.m., and sometimes five times a night. I was up and down throughout the night, very seldom getting sleep. She would say her legs and feet hurt, her hat came off, she was wet, or she would say, "What can I do now?" I think she wanted attention at night because she slept a lot during the day. I enjoyed caring for my Mom. She now had become my baby.

One morning after no sleep, I woke up with a terrible headache. The TV was on a gospel station, and the preacher said, "Someone out there has a bad headache, and their name starts with an S." He said, "Be healed in Jesus' name," and the headache left. Praise God, He is a miracle worker!

The saints would often text me or call me with great words of encouragement. Missionary Verma Harvey would text me encouraging words or songs every day. Mother Gloria Sanders texted often, and Evangelist Sharon Williams, Bishop Timothy Smith, and others called often. I don't want to call names because so many kept up with me; even General Supervisor Barbara McCoo Lewis and Mother Rosetta Watts texted me words of encouragement. I was also often part of the Williams Temple prayer line. Of course, my husband always encouraged me daily. I thank God for the prayer warriors who held us up in prayer daily.

On June 1, the health department came and tested us again. With the June 3 results, I was cleared, testing negative, but Mom was still positive. She was so sad, still testing positive with the third test and after thirty-three days. She said, "I am old. That's why I still have the virus." I told her, "God will heal you."

One night my Mom coughed so bad she seemed to be losing consciousness and looking faint. I thought she was going to die that night. I was so sad. My sisters and I talked and decided to release her if it was her time to go. She lay there, eyes closed, looking pale. I said, "Mom, are you ready to go to heaven?" She opened her eyes wide, looked at me, and said, "Are you?" I said yes. Then she started preaching: "He's coming like a thief in the night. We know not the day or the hour. But we got to be ready." I said, "That's right."

After she tested positive three times, we began to search for a nursing home that took in COVID-19 patients. At this point, Bishop Wooten said, "What is the family going to do if she tests positive a fourth time?" I knew his long-suffering was running out. I had three social workers helping to search. It seemed as though no one was taking new clients. Finally, a social worker called and said she thought she had found a nursing home in Richmond, Virginia. She told me to call them. I called, and they were very positive. They agreed to admit her on June 11 at 4 p.m. to the COVID-19 unit. They said when she tested negative, they would move her to the non-COVID-19 ward step-down unit.

This was a large, gorgeous, rich-looking nursing home. They had lost some patients to the virus when it first came on the scene. They thought it was the flu. But since that time, they had revamped and reorganized in CDC and state compliance and had a 4.5 rating out of 5 points. We knew this was the place for our dear mom, an hour and a half from family. Our search was finally over.

I told the Lord I did not want to go home with Mom still positive. I stood on the word of I John 5:15 which says, "And if we know that he hear us, whatsoever we ask, we know that we have the petitions that we desired of him." They tested Mom for the virus again on June 16, and on June 17, she tested *negative*. Thank You, Jesus! I went to Rite-Aid to be tested again also before going home, and I tested negative again, also on June 17. Also, my family back home in St. Louis, Bishop, Grace, Sarah, and Kim, went to our adult daycare for free testing. All tested negative on the seventeenth of June. We all tested *negative* on June 17. The number *17* means victory and perfection. Thank God for the victory!

Mom tested positive for forty-nine days. I took care of her for thirty-five days and returned home after forty-four days in Virginia on June 20. The number *49* is a symbol of security and progress and represents continuity, steadiness, and persistence. It is a message that means your angels are with you as you step through a new door of opportunity. Mom's angels were truly with her at ninety-three years of age.

We had a "window visit" with Mom on June 20 on my way to the airport to return to St. Louis. She was happy and looked good. She said, "Shirley stayed with me a long time" and smiled. It was a long journey, and I would do it all once again to help my Mom. She was a jewel, a true saint of God.

Satan attacked Grace, my husband, my mom, and me, but God triumphed over the enemy and defeated him with a crushing blow against COVID 19. Thank God for the victory!

About eight months, after Mom was delivered from COVID-19 and entered the Nursing Home, on February 1, 2021, I got a call that Mom was not eating due to dementia and had dropped to only 59 pounds, skin and bones. I flew home and they permitted me to come into the nursing home to visit her. The Family had window visits with her, and she was so happy. She ate for me, and I was so glad. But as I sat by her bedside on February 4th, she looked towards heaven, waved her hand in the air and said a few words in another language. She looked up and saw the angles of God coming to carry her home. I began to pray for her, to sing songs and quote scriptures. She continued to look up with her mouth opened,, and finally she stopped breathing. I knew that to be absent from the body is to be present with the Lord. Heaven had welcomed her home at 94 years old. It was a sad day for the family, but we gave God the glory.

Chapter 5

Ten Steps to Victory Over COVID-19 or Any Other Problems

You can break through to victory over COVID-19 or any other attack of the enemy. The enemy will attack through sickness, finances, family, job, or other areas. The steps you take are the same.

Step 1: Recognize the source of opposition as being Satan.
God is not responsible for sickness, accidents, death, catastrophe, etc.

"The thief cometh not, but for to steal, to kill, and to destroy: I am come that they might have life, and that they might have it more abundantly" (John 10:10).

Stand your ground. Do not allow Satan to defeat you. Wrap yourself in the promises of God and rest in the Lord. Resist fear and doubt. Remember, we have authority over Satan and can be victorious through our Lord Jesus Christ.

Step 2: Be sure the promises of God cover the things you are asking and believing for.
Faith is based on God's Word: "So then faith cometh by hearing, and hearing by the word of God" (Romans 10:17).

Do the promises of God cover what you are believing for: healing, finances, deliverance, peace, joy, salvation, companionship? Find the scriptures that promise the things you are praying for.

Step 3: Be sure you are not living in sin.

Sin is a hindrance to faith and your prayers; "But if we walk in the light, as He is in the light, we have fellowship one with another, and the blood of Jesus Christ His Son cleanseth us from all sin" (1 John 1:7).

"And when ye stand praying, forgive, if ye have ought against any: that your Father also which is in heaven may forgive you your trespasses" (Mark 11:25); therefore, Be quick to forgive, quick to repent, and quick to believe God.

Step 4: Be sure no doubt or unbelief is permitted in your life concerning the promises of God.

The devil will try to hinder your blessings from manifesting.

"Fight the good fight of faith, lay hold on eternal life"… (1 Timothy 6:12);

Faith always has a good report. Speak those things that be not as though they were.

"And they brought up an evil report of the land which they had searched unto the children of Israel"… (Numbers 13:32); this report was from negative thinkers.

Thinking faith thoughts and speaking faith words will lead the heart out of defeat and into victory.

Repeat these faith-filled words aloud:

Faith always has a good report.
I walk by faith and not by sight.
I am a faith person.
I refuse doubt.
I refuse fear.
I am a faith child of a faith God.
My faith works.
I always have a good report.
I refuse an evil report.
I am on God's side.
I belong to God.
I serve God.
I am a child of God.
I believe God.
I believe God that it shall be even as it was told me in His Holy Word.
God's Word cannot fail.
I cannot fail.
I am standing on the Word.
I am standing on the promises.

Step 5: Sincerely desire the benefit you have asked of God.

Prayer cannot override a person's desire or will. God made man and gave him a choice, a will of his own. You cannot get someone healed while they are believing they are going to die. You must get them to agree with you and with God's Word.

Therefore, "I say unto you, what things soever ye desire, when ye pray, believe that ye receive them, and ye shall have them" (Mark 11:24).

Matthew 18:19 states, "Again I say unto you, That if two of you shall agree on earth as touching any thing that they shall ask, it shall be done for them of my Father which is in heaven".

Step 6: Ask God in faith, nothing wavering, believing that what is asked is yours.

Pray to receive something from God.

"Therefore, I say unto you, What things soever ye desire, when ye pray, believe that ye receive them, and ye shall have them" (Mark 11:24).

Believe—believe that you will receive the things you are praying for.

Stand your ground and do not waver; "If any of you lack wisdom, let him ask of God, that giveth to all men liberally, and upbraideth not; and it shall be given him. But let him ask in faith, nothing wavering. For he that wavereth is like a wave of the sea driven with the wind and tossed. For let not that man think that he shall receive any thing of the Lord" (James 1:5-7).

Step 7: Do not tolerate for one single moment a thought to the contrary of what you are believing God for.

"Casting down imaginations, and every high thing that exalteth itself against the knowledge of God, and bringing into captivity every thought to the obedience of Christ" is what Paul advises (2 Corinthians 10:5).

- Never permit a mental picture of failure to remain in your mind.
- Rebuke doubt. Get your mind on the answer.

— Stay away from all places, things, and people that do not support your affirmation that God has answered your prayer.

Govern your thoughts according to this: "Finally brethren, whatsoever things are true, whatsoever things are honest, whatsoever things are just, whatsoever things are pure, whatsoever things are lovely, whatsoever things are of good report: if there be any virtue, and if there be any praise, think on these things" (Philipians. 4:8).

Step 8: Count the things done that you have asked for.
We need Abraham's type of faith:

— Galatians 3:29: "And if ye be Christ's then are ye Abraham's seed, and heirs according to the promise."
— Galatians 3:7: "They which are of faith, the same are the children of Abraham."
— Romans 4:17:… "And calleth those things which be not as though they were."

The principles of faith work in any realm: healing, financial, spiritual, etc. We walk by faith and not by sight (2 Cor. 5:7). Faith gives substance to things not seen (Heb. 11:1). What if the man at the pool of Bethesda had fainted during those thirty-eight years? He would have missed his season and not received his healing (John 5:1–15).

The new birth is based on faith (Rom. 10:9–10). A person must confess he is saved before it ever happens. Anything we get from God comes the same way, through confession.

Step 9: Give glory to God even before your request comes into manifestation.

Abraham gave God the glory before it manifested: "He staggered not at the promise of God through unbelief; but was strong in faith, *giving glory to God*; and being fully persuaded that, what he had promised, he was also able to perform" (Romans 4:20–21).

You thank God for it after you pray for it (Philipians 4:6). Thinking faith thoughts and speaking faith words leads the heart out of defeat and into victory.

Step 10: By faith, act as though you have received what you have asked for.

Act like you are healed, prospering, delivered, etc., not in presumption, but in faith.

Put up a fight for what belongs to you.

"If ye abide in me, and my words abide in you, ye shall ask what you will, and it shall be done unto you, says" (John 15:7).

By faith, you have the breakthrough to victory over COVID-19, over all sicknesses and diseases, and over every attack of the enemy!

Chapter 6

Deliverance in Your Praise

Whatever you are going through, COVID-19 or any other affliction, there's deliverance in your praise. "By him there let us offer the sacrifice of praise to God continually, that is, the fruit of our lips giving thanks to his name" (Hebrews 13:15).

What is praise? Praise is the act of making positive statements about God; to admire, to command, to extol, to lift Him up, to magnify, to exalt His name.

Hallelujah is the highest praise. We may praise people, places, and things, but today we are praising God. Why praise God? The Bible says in Psalm 105:6, "Let everything that hath breath praise the Lord. Praise ye the Lord." God created man to give Him praise. Psalm 107:31 says, "Oh, that men would praise the Lord for His goodness and for his wonderful works to the children of men!"

First Peter 2:9 says, "But ye are a chosen generation, a royal priesthood, a holy nation, a peculiar people, that ye should show forth the praises of him who hath called you out of darkness into his marvelous light."

God inhabits, or lives, in the praises of His people. God's address is Praise Boulevard. Praise builds a throne for God to come into the midst of His people to bring healing and deliverance.

> **P**raise
> **R**eaches
> **A**tmosphere
> **I**nvokes
> **S**piritual
> **E**ncounter

Praise is what we do when we want to be close to God. Praise elevates us into God's presence and power. Praise ushers in the peace and glory of God.

Praise is your gate pass. Psalm 100:4 says, "Enter into His gates with thanksgiving and into His courts with praise: be thankful unto Him, and bless His name."

Anyone can praise Him when things are going well. But can you praise Him in the midst of your fiery tests and trial, sickness in body, bills due, job problems, family problems? Then can you praise Him?

What should we praise Him for?

I Thessalonians 5:18 says, "In everything give thanks, for this is the will of God in Christ Jesus concerning you." It doesn't say to give thanks *for* everything, but *in* everything. Psalm 107:31–32 says, "Oh, that men would praise God for His goodness, for His wonderful works to the children of men."

How long should we praise Him? Hebrews 13:15 tells us to offer praise to God continually, and Psalm 34:1 says to bless the Lord at all times.

There is victory and dynamite in your praise. Your praise will ambush the devil. Let's look at some biblical examples. In

2 Chronicles 20, the Ammonites came against Jehoshaphat to battle, and he needed a miracle. He began to fast and pray and seek God.

Second Chronicles 20:15b says, "Thus saith the Lord unto you, be not afraid nor dismayed for reasons of this great multitude; for the battle is not yours but God's." Verse 17a reads, "Ye shall not need to fight in this battle: set yourselves, stand you still and see the salvation of the Lord with you."

Verse 21 follows with, "And when he had consulted with the people he appointed singers to the Lord, and that should praise the beauty of holiness, as they went out before the army, and to say, Praise the Lord; for his mercy endures forever."

Finally, 2 Chronicles 20:22 records, "And when they began to sing and to praise, the Lord set ambushments against the children of Ammon, Moab and Mount Seir, which were come against Judah; and they were smitten." Jehoshaphat defeated the enemy with praise! Praise will always put the devil on the run.

Another example is found in Acts 16. Paul and Silas were locked in jail for preaching the gospel and casting the devil out of a damsel. Acts 16:25–26 says, "And at midnight Paul and Silas prayed, and sang praises to God: and the prisoners heard them. And suddenly there was a great earthquake, so that the foundations of the prison were shaken and immediately all the doors were opened, and every one's bands were loosed." The jailhouse began to rock, Paul's and Silas's chains were loosed, prisoners were set free, revival broke out, and the keeper of the jail and his house were saved. When you pray and praise, God will loose all those around you and bring deliverance.

No one can say they do not have faith. For the Bible says in…Romans 12:3" – For I say, through the grace given unto me, to every man that is among you, not to think of himself more highly than he ought to think; but to think soberly, according as God hath dealt to every man the measure of faith."

When you praise God, miracles will happen suddenly:

—Walls will come down.
—The mouths of lions will be shut.
—Fiery darts will be quenched.
—Blind eyes will open.
—"Red Seas" will part.
—Tumors will dissolve.
—Captives will be loosed.
—The dead will be raised.
—COVID-19 will be rebuked and eliminated.
Praise Him in the good times.
Praise Him in the bad times.
Let everything that hath breath praise ye the Lord.
Praise will defeat COVID-19.
My family and I are living testimonies that praise will bring you out!

Chapter 7

Just a Test

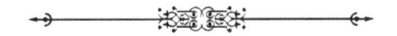

COVID-19: Don't panic, it's only a test.
Bills due: Don't panic, it's only a test.
Sick in body: Don't panic, it's only a test.
Job problems: Don't panic, it's only a test.
Children problems: Don't panic, it's only a test.
Family issues: Don't panic, it's only a test.

"Beloved, think it not strange concerning the fiery trial which is to try you, as though some strange thing happened unto you. But rejoice inasmuch as ye are partakers of Christ's sufferings, that when this glory shall be revealed, ye may be glad with exceeding joy" (1 Pet. 4:12–13). Be encouraged...This too shall pass.

What is panic? It is fear affecting an individual, widespread alarm. Don't have a panic attack when tests come your way.

What is a test? A test is a trial, or examination. If you fail your test, it's coming up again. If you panic during your test, that will lead to fainting, giving up, or losing heart. Signs of natural fainting are dizziness, blurred vision, slumping, falling, passing out. People do strange things when they become faint. Esau came in from the field and was faint. He sold his birthright for a bowl of beans. Don't faint (Genesis 25:30)! Proverbs 24:10 says, "If thou faint in the day of adversity, thy strength is small." Isaiah 40:29–31 says, "He giveth power to the faint and to him that hath no might he increaseth strength."

Luke 18:1 says, "And he spake a parable unto them to the end, that men ought to always pray and not faint." God inhabits, or lives, in the praises of His people. God's address is Praise Boulevard. Praise builds a throne for God to come into the midst of His people to bring healing and deliverance.

The opposite of fainting is reviving. Lord, revive us again!

Whatever you do, don't faint now. It's due season. The windows of heaven are open. Don't panic, it's just a test! Galatians 6:9 says, "And let us not be weary in well doing; for in due season, we shall reap if we faint not." The devil wants you to panic, faint, and give up just before your due season, but it's your time to be blessed in the midst of the test. Don't panic, don't panic—it's just a test!

Ecclesiastes 3:1 reminds us, "To everything, there is a season and a time to every purpose under the heaven—a time to be born and a time to die...a time to plant and a time to pluck up...a time to get and time to lose."

Understand the season you are in. Something good is coming out of this test.

For example you have planted; now it's time to reap the harvest (e.g., in farming, you plant, fertilize, chop, water, and chop again until finally the cotton is ready to pick). You've sown in righteousness. Now it's time to reap.

Look at the positive. We are in lockdown with Jesus, lockdown with our families, lockdown in resting and sleeping, lockdown in bonding and communicating. There are no fast foods, and we are eating healthy. We are exercising, not spending a lot of money. Don't panic during your test. Blessing is nigh thee!

But why do you have to be tested and tested and tested? Your faith must be tested to show you where you are. God knows. For example, Abraham, on Mount Moriah, had to be tested, and he passed the test (Gen. 22:1–19). When you are tested, God brags on you: "Have you considered my servant Job?"

Job lost everything: children, cattle, and land. His wife turned on him, and he was sick unto death. However, his later end was greater than his beginning. He had to be tested; he passed the test and did not sin (Job 6:1–2). Your test will take you to another level of power and authority.

For example, Joseph went from the pit, to Potiphar's house, to prison, to the palace. Each test took him to another level, until he ended up in the palace (Gen. 37–50). Jesus was tested in the wilderness, and He came out walking in power. He said, "It is written," and defeated satan (Matthew 4:1–8).

There must be a death before a resurrection. If there is no trial, there is no triumph; no test, no testimony; no cross, no crown. How can you pass the test without panic and fainting? Stand on 1 Corinthians 10:13: *"There hath no temptation taken you but such as is common to man, but God is faithful, who will not suffer you to be tempted above that you are able, but will with the temptation also make a way of escape that ye may be able to bear it".*

A person whose behavior is out of control achieves nothing.

What if the woman with the issue had panicked and not pressed her way forward? She would not have received healing (Luke 8:43-48).

What if the Syrophoenician woman had not been persistent? Her son would not have been healed (Mark 24-30).

What if blind Bartimaeus had not cried out "Jesus, have mercy on me"? (Mark 10:47) But Jesus stood still and told the men to "bring him to me."

Jesus asked the man what does he want? Bartimaeus answered, my sight, and Jesus healed him." (Mark 10:49a-51).

What do you do when tests hit on the right, the left, the front, and the back? When sickness, money, job, or family problems come, what do you do?

Obey James 1:2-3 "Count it all joy when ye fall into divers temptations, knowing this that the trying of your faith worketh patience."

First Peter 1:7 says "that the trial of your faith, being much more precious than gold that perished, though it be tried with fire, might be found unto praise and honour and glory at the appearing of Jesus Christ."

God knows how much you can bear. He will not put more on you than you can bear. He knows when to bring you out of the test you are in right now.

Like gold in the fire, all imperfections are burned off. He molds you on the potter's wheel, takes off imperfections, and shapes you into His image.

A great silversmith was once asked a question: "How do you know when the silver piece is complete and ready to come forth?" He replied, "When I can look at it and see the image of myself in the silver." Jesus is looking to see at what point during your test He can see Himself in you. The silversmith also said, "When I hit the silver piece and it sings, I know it's ready and completed." Can you sing and praise God when hit with adversity?

Don't panic during lockdown in the pandemic. In lockdown, it is time to do the following:

> **L** — Listen to God's voice and reflect.
> **O** — Obey His Words and teachings.
> **C** — Call on Jesus' name, and be calm.
> **K** — Know what is the purpose of this all.
> **D** — Dwell in His presence, but don't panic.
> **O** — Offer prayer for everyone's safety.
> **W** — Wait and be patient; this too shall pass.
> **N** — Nurture your personal relationship with God.

Don't panic in lockdown. It's just a test!

Chapter 8

Contend for the Faith

Jude 1:3 tells us, "Beloved, when I gave all diligence to write unto you of the common salvation, it was needful for me to write unto you, and exhort you that ye should earnestly contend for the faith which was once delivered unto the saints." Your faith in God will overcome COVID-19 or any other problem But you have to put up a fight.

What is Faith? Hebrews 11:1 – "Faith is the substance of things hoped for, the evidence of things not seen: "Faith is total, complete trust in God; Believing, relying, serving, and depending on God is Faith. Faith is knowing he will come through. No one can say they do not have faith. For the Bible says in…Romans 12:3" – For I say, through the grace given unto me, to every man that is among you, not to think of himself more highly than he ought to think; but to think soberly, according as God hath dealt to every man the measure of faith."

We are saved by Faith. Ephesians 2:8 – "For by grace are ye saved, through faith, and that not of yourselves; it is the gift of God."

The same faith that saved us, also heals us and works for us in other areas. Faith in God can deliver from COVID-19 and any other diseases.

How do we get more faith? Romans 10:17 states, "So then faith cometh by hearing, and hearing by the word of God". You must hear the preached word, and you must hear yourself say the word: <u>Say:</u> I am healed, I am blessed, I am prosperous, and victorious, etc. What Are You Saying? You must say the Word! Whose report will you believe? I believe the report of the Lord. God is a healer and a mighty deliverer.

Why do we need faith? We need faith to please God.

Hebrews 11:6 says, "But without faith it is impossible to please him: for he that cometh to God must believe that he is, and that he is a rewarder of them that diligently seek him." We need faith to be saved, healed, and have victory over satan. Our shield of faith quenches fiery darts of the devil.

Anything other than faith is sin. Doubt is sin; children of Israel missed the Promise Land because of unbelief, complaining and murmuring. Let us not murmer and complain, but let, us hold on by Faith and trust God.

How can I receive by faith? First, Believe. When you pray, believe that the over 2000 promises in the word are true. Mark 11:24 reads, "What things soever ye desire, when you pray believe that ye receive them, and ye shall have them. "Faith moves God, not tears, begging, or pleading. You must act like it's already done. You must go from expectation to manifestation, and don't abort the baby!

Believing for a car – buy car mats!
Believing for a house – get some furniture!
Believing for marriage – get a hope chest with your negligee!

You need to use your Mountain Moving Mustard Seed Faith and believe God!

Put on your faith glasses and began to see through eyes of faith. See your healing; see your miracle!

Faith sees…

- Spring in winter
- Showers in drought
- Solutions, not problems
- Glory not gloom
- Peace in turmoil
- Light in darkness
- Joy in sorrow
- Healing in sickness
- Freedom in bondage
- Money in poverty

Faith…

- Obeys the commands of god
- Believes the word of god
- Stands on the promises of god
- Relies on the mercies of god
- Trusts the wisdom of god
- Accepts the will of god

God honors faith

What faith speaks – God hears
What faith requests – God gives
What faith wants – God grants
What faith believes – God delivers
What faith asks – God answers
What faith demands – God supplies
What faith expects – God does

What faith desires – God submits
What faith trusts – God honors
What faith treads – God walks
What faith moves – God ministers
What faith knocks – God opens
What faith seeks – God reveals
What faith purposes – God delights
What faith requires – God satisfies
What faith insists – God responds
What faith declares – God upholds
What faith claims – God fulfills
What faith grasps – God extends
What faith accepts – God offers
What faith needs – God provides
What faith visualizes – God materializes
What faith anticipates – God assures
What faith adventures – God leads
What faith lives – God inspires
What faith receives – God blesses
What faith obeys – God performs
What faith tugs – God yields
What faith leads – God guides
What faith listens – God speaks

So have faith in God!

"**Through Faith** miracles were wrought in the Bible and **through Faith** God is still working miracles. The devil is defeated, God is exalted and Jesus is Lord!"

"**Through faith** we understand that the worlds was framed by the word of God, so that things which are seen were not made of things which do appear."

"**By faith** Abel offered unto God a more excellent sacrifice than Cain, by which he obtained witness that he was righteous, God testifying of his gifts: and by it he being dead yet speaketh."

"**By faith** Enoch was translated that he should not see death; and was not found, because God had translated him: for before his translation he had this testimony, that he pleased God."

"But without faith it is impossible to please him; for he that cometh to God must believe that he is, and that he is a rewarder of them that diligently seek him."

"**By faith** Noah, being warned of God of things not seen as yet, moved with fear, prepared an ark to the saving of his house; by the which he condemned the world, and became heir of the righteousness which is **by faith**."

"**By faith** Abraham, when he was called to go out into a place which he should after receive for an inheritance, obeyed; and he went out, not knowing whither he went."

"**By faith** he sojourned in the land of promise, as in a strange country, dwelling in tabernacles with Isaac and Jacob, the heirs with him of the same promise." Hebrew 11:3-9

Chapter 9

40 Day Worldwide Fast and Prayer Against COVID 19

Bishop J. Drew Sheard, Presiding of the Church of God in Christ, and Bishop Lawrence M. Wooten, Second Assistant Presiding Bishop of the Church of God In Christ, called for a Worldwide 40 Day Fast and Prayer Against Covid-19, February 1, 2022 through March 12, 2022. See flyers on pages 55, 56.

II Chronicles 7:14 says, "If my people, which are called by my name, shall humble themselves, and pray, and seek my face, and turn from their wicked ways; then will I hear from heaven, and will forgive their sin, and will heal their land". Matthew 17:21 says, "Howbeit this kind goeth not out but by prayer and fasting".

People all over the world began to fast and pray against covid-19. They undertook different types of fasts to defeat the demonic virus, as on the flyer.

Many called for various prayer services and conference call prayer lines, praying with one accord, worldwide and in all denominations. Many COGIC Leaders, family, Saints and friends died as a result of covid-19. We decided enough is enough! We must put this demon on the run. United we Stand, divided we fall.

COGIC churches are established in 112 countries, and they were all asked to join in the 40 day fast and prayer. Much unity was exemplified worldwide, and results were evident after a few weeks of fasting and praying. See article on page 57-58, "COVID CASES Plummet all across the US", Feb. 17, 2022, New York Times.

God answered the prayers of the righteous as the virus greatly decreased, deaths decreased, hospitalizations decreased and many people worldwide were taken off the ventilators. This was all the result of fervent prayer and prayer and fasting worldwide.

Let's Examine Fasting and Prayer

WHAT IS FASTING?

> Fasting is abstinence from food or anything of nutritional value. There are a lot of misconceptions about fasting. Based on research, doctors indicate that fasting is good for the physical body. The Bible lets us know that fasting is good for the SPIRIT part of man. As we fast and pray, it prepares our heart in humility, it whips the flesh into line and helps to get rid of unbelief. Our main objective is to seek God in prayer and the humiliation of the flesh through fasting.
>
> Fasting is a symbol of mourning, going down into repentance and chastening of the heart. One of the main purposes of the fast is to forsake

all pleasures, of which, the eating pleasure is the key stone to all other pleasures.

TYPES OF FASTS:

There are many different types of fasts. The type fast you go on should be directed by God. Some of the types of fasts are as follows:

1. No food or water
2. Water only-no food
3. No pleasant bread (food which you do not like)
4. One meal a day
5. Juice and water only

WHY SHOULD I FAST?

Why fast? Because the Bible says so, and it is the final authority. Jesus fasted often, so what about us? In Matthew 9:14, "when the bridegroom is taken, then shall they fast." The bridegroom has been taken, so now it is time to fast. The three foundations of the church are GIVING, PRAYER AND FASTING. Matthew 6:1-18

Fasting and prayer helps to get rid carnality. Fasting puts self in the background and the SPIRIT man becomes more sensitive to the voice of God. The same door that closes carnality opens up the spiritual – FASTING.

There is no habit or weakness that can survive a siege of prayer and fasting plus obedience to the word. There are many biblical examples of those in the Bible who fasted:

- Moses – Exodus 24:18, 34:27,28
- Daniel – Daniel 10:2
- Ezra – Ezra 8:21-23
- Esther – Esther 4:16
- Anna – Luke 2:36
- Cornelius – Acts 10:36
- Saul – Acts 9:7
- Paul – Acts 27:21-33
- Jesus – Matthew 4:23, 24

Prayer and fasting are the combination needed for THIS KIND. It's the need that calls for the affliction of our body and the determination to hear from God, and cast out demonic spirits.

Matthew 17:16-21, "And I brought him to thy disciples, and they could not cure him. Then Jesus answered and said, O faithless and perverse generation, how long shall I be with you? How long shall I suffer you? Bring him hither to me. And Jesus rebuked the devil; and he departed out of him: and the child was cured from that very hour. Then came the disciples to Jesus apart, and said, Why could not we cast him out? And Jesus said unto them, Because of your unbelief: for verily I say unto you, if ye have faith as a grain of mustard seed, ye shall say unto this mountain, Remove hence to yonder place; and it shall remove; and nothing shall be impossible unto you. Howbeit this kind goeth not out but by prayer and fasting."

Fasting is letting go the visible to get in touch with the invisible. It may be food or any other enjoyment of life that we deny ourselves. Fasting crucifies the flesh and puts our spirit in touch with God.

Matthew 6:16-18, "Moreover when ye fast, be not, as the hypocrites, of a sad countenance: for they disfigure their faces, that they may appear unto men to fast. Verily I say unto you, They have their reward. But thou, when thou fastest, anoint thine head, and wash they face; That thou appear not unto men to fast, but unto thy Father which is in secret: and they Father, which seeth in secret, shall reward thee openly." When we fast the right way mountains will move and prayers will be answered.

When should we fast and what is fasting for? Let's examine, examples from God's Word.

Joel 1:14, "Sanctify ye a fast, call a solemn assembly, gather the elders and all the inhabitants of the land into the house of the Lord your God, and cry unto the Lord," We find here we are to call for a fast to declare our dedication or to show God we mean business, It's a way of turning to the Lord. Joel 2:12, "Therefore also now, saith the Lord, Turn ye even to me with all your heart, and with fasting, and with weeping, and with morning."

When something needs to change, we fast to promote a reformation.

Nehemiah 1:3-4, "And they said unto me, The remnant that are left of the captivity there in the province are in great affliction and reproach: the wall of Jerusalem also is broken down, and the gates thereof are burned with fire.

And it came to pass, when I heard these words, that I sat down and wept, and mourned certain days, and fasted, and prayed before the God of heaven." If you are tired of the oppressing circumstances, it's time to fast and pray. It's time to fast when pending judgment is about to fall. Jonah 3:5, "So the people of Ninevah believed God, and proclaimed a fast, and put on sackcloth, from the greatest of them even to the least of them." The results of their fasting, their lives were spared.

King David also tried to release God's mercy for his baby by fasting. Even though it was not to be, David knew the principal of fasting. II Samuel 12:16, "David therefore besought God for the child; and David fasted, and went in, and lay all night upon the earth."

When we need direction and are determined to hear from God we should fast and pray. But when everything is running smoothly, we should also fast as part of our ministry and service to God.

TIPS ON FASTING

During your fast, set aside specific and significant time to worship and seek God in prayer. Plan ahead so your time can be unhurried and conductive to enjoying the Lord. Many people begin this time by repenting of any sins the Holy Spirit brings to mind and asking for God's forgiveness. This is essential to ensure that sin is not hindering your communication with God.

Then plan time to make your requests known to God and to seek His will. Take breaks to study scripture passages you have chosen. Don't rush your time with God. Take time to listen. Keep a notebook and pen nearby to record the ideas, insights, directions and instructions He impresses on your mind. When fasting, you can more easily hear God.

Continue to drink plenty of water. Apple or watermelon juice is a great morale booster. Sleep early – the first few days of the fast are usually the most challenging. Persevere through this period. Consult your doctor if you are unsure of any headaches or bodily reactions.

Breaking the fast may require as much discipline as beginning it. During the fast, your stomach contracts and your body's digestive and elimination systems rest. The longer you fast, the more time the digestive organs need to reactivate before functioning at full speed.

If you plan to fast only a day or two at a time, it is best to end the fast with a small glass of fruit juice as your first meal. Gradually introduce small amounts of easily digestible foods such as yogurt, soup, fresh fruit, and cooked vegetables.

If your fast lasts longer than a few days, you should continue with juices for a day or more before gradually introducing more substantial foods like yogurt, soup and fruit. Be sure you introduce new foods in small quantities and that you chew it well. You should stop eating at the slightest sensation of fullness.

If fasting only a few days at a time, ending the fast should be easier. If you have built up to and desire to fast longer, you should consult your physician and review a health book on fasting.

It takes time to build our spiritual fasting muscles. If you fail to make it through your first fast, do not be discouraged. You may have tried to fast too long the first time, or you may need to strengthen your understanding and resolve. Keep trying until you do succeed. God will honor you for your faithfulness.

Fasting is a way God's people have humbled themselves before Him for more than three thousand years! Jesus, David, and many other followers of our God have gone without food to worship and pray to the one who supplies all our needs.

For healthy individuals, no harm results from short-term fasting. The average healthy person can go-without food between 21 and 40 or more days before the body begins to eliminate vital tissue (starvation). **Consult your physician before beginning any fast lasting longer then three days**. If you have underlying health conditions such as pregnancy, anemia, behavioral disorders or other chronic health problems, you should never fast without consulting a physician first.

We thank God for the 40 day worldwide fast and prayer that made a difference in the COVID-19 attack upon the world. Many lives were spared as a result of prayer and fasting.

GOD AGAINST COVID-19

CHURCH OF GOD IN CHRIST, INC.
Presiding Bishop J. Drew Sheard Calls For
Worldwide Prayer & Fasting to Defeat the Coronavirus

40 DAYS OF PRAYER & FASTING
FEB 1 – MAR 12
BEGINNING & ENDING AT MIDNIGHT
Matthew 17:21 | 2 Chronicles 7:14

2 Chronicles 7:14 – "If my people, which are called by my name, shall humble themselves, and pray, and seek my face, and turn from their wicked ways; then will I hear from heaven, and will forgive their sin, and will heal their land."

Matthew 17:21 - "Howbeit, this kind goeth not out, but by prayer and fasting."

The coronavirus has taken over the world and killed millions. If we unite in fasting & prayer worldwide, God will deliver and loose the captives.

Let us continue to adhere to Presiding Bishop J. Drew Sheard's 22-day call to prayer, fasting & rededication - extended to March 12, 2022

HOW TO FAST:
Different types of fasts:
- No food - water only
- Water & juice only
- Eat one meal a day
- The Daniel Fast

- *Before The Fast:* Repent & be sure you are saved! (Rom 10:9-10); (Ps 66:18)
- *During The Fast:* Consecrate yourself, be prayerful, read your Bible, and thank God for the victory over COVID-19 & its variants and strains. (Isaiah 58:6-11)
- *After The Fast:* Break your fast slowly and give God the glory for a mighty deliverance.

Coordinator:
Bishop Lawrence M. Wooten, Sr.
2nd Assistant Presiding Bishop of the COGIC, Inc.

COGIC LEGAL DISCLAIMER: "We do not recommend anything that contradicts the advice of your physician. Please consult with your physician or medical professional before beginning the fast."

CHURCH OF GOD IN CHRIST, INC.
BISHOP J. DREW SHEARD - PRESIDING BISHOP & CHIEF APOSTLE
Soaring Higher With
FASTING and PRAYING
And Jesus said unto them, Because of your unbelief: for verily I say unto you, If ye have faith as a grain of mustard seed, ye shall say unto this mountain, Remove hence to yonder place; and it shall remove; and nothing shall be impossible unto you. Howbeit this kind goeth not out but by prayer and fasting. - MATTHEW 17:20-21
And his name through faith in his name hath made this man strong, whom ye see and know: yea, the faith which is by him hath given him this perfect soundness in the presence of you all. - ACTS 3:16
MARCH 1 | SUNDAY SCHOOL
- UNBELIEF is crushed by prayer and fasting
- Our seed of faith is lifeblood to healing-wholeness
- Holy Obedience positions us for strength
- Accessing the Faith lever- Nothing is Impossible
MARCH 4 | DEPARTMENT OF EVANGELISM
- Our faith reverses the curse
- Praying-Speaking against Pandemic now
- Our Faith filled words turns the situation around
MARCH 8 | PASTORS AND ELDERS
- Stand fast "Never waver" Always believe God
- Breaking the enemy's grip-in Jesus name
- We pray for perfect soundness in achievements
MARCH 11 | ADJUTANCY
- The Armor of his righteousness covers us
- The SOARING IN HIS PRESENCE-WITH FASTING AND PRAYER
zoom
TUESDAYS & FRIDAYS
12PM EST | 11AM CST | 10AM MST | 9AM PST
Webinar ID: 815 9706 8970
Passcode: 111035
DIAL IN (US)
669-900-6833, 253-215-8782, 346-248-7799
301-715-8592, 312-626-6799, or 929-205-6099
COORDINATOR:
Bishop Lawrence M. Wooten, Sr.
2nd Assistant Presiding Bishop

Feb 17, 2022–Health

COVID cases plummet all across the U.S.

Data: N.Y. Times; Cartogram: Kavya Beheraj/Axios

Feb. 2 to Feb. 15, 2022

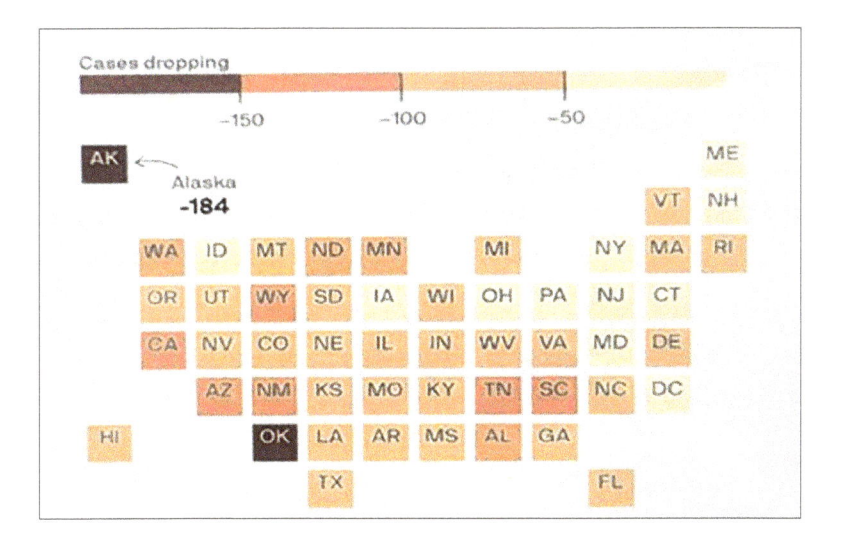

COVID cases are plummeting across the U.S., in some places even falling to relatively manageable levels. But deaths remain stubbornly high.

The big picture: States and cities of all political stripes are removing mask and vaccine mandates as the Omicron variant loses steam, though in some regions there's still a ways to go before the virus is truly under control.

By the numbers: Nationwide, the U.S. is now averaging roughly 140,000 new COVID cases per day — a 64% drop over the past two weeks. The pace of new infections is declining in every state.

But there's a difference between a *declining* number of cases and a *small* number of cases.

- Some regions of the U.S. have achieved both: COVID cases have fallen all the way down to levels that experts consider at least relatively safe.
- New York, New Jersey and Connecticut are all averaging fewer than 25 new cases per 100,000 people per day. So is Washington, D.C., and Maryland is doing even better, at just 12 cases per day for every 100,000 residents.
- Much of the U.S., however, isn't quite there yet. In Alaska, for example, new cases are dropping significantly, but the state is still averaging 100 cases per 100,000 people, the highest rate in the country.

What we're watching: Omicron is clearly on its way out, and the overall situation in the U.S. is getting much better. But unvaccinated Americans remain at risk for serious illness and death.

- The virus is killing more than 2,300 Americans per day, on average. That's a 13% improvement over the past two weeks, but still adds up to a significant amount of preventable death and suffering.

Chapter 10

Summary

Many are the afflictions of the righteous, but God delivers us out of them all. Don't panic during your tests and trials. Hold your head up and go through with the victory, knowing that God will sustain you and bring you out, more than a conqueror. My family and I went through that COVID-19 dilemma and came out without even the "smell of smoke". The weapons were formed, but they did not prosper.

"Therefore, my beloved brethren, be ye steadfast, unmoveable, always abounding in the work of the Lord, foreasmuch as ye know that your labour is not in vain in the Lord" (1 Corinthians 15:58).

Be ye steadfast in your... Fasting and prayer, In the Word, In your faith, In your praise.

Cast not away your confidence, and put your trust in God. God cannot fail; He cannot deny and He cannot lie. I see you coming out with your hands up, shouting the victory, with pep in your step and praise on your lips. Delay does not mean denial. Just hold on, and the appointed time will come. Though it tarry, wait on it. Through it all, I've learned to trust in Jesus and take Him at His Word. I've learned to rest in Him and cast all my cares upon Him. I know that if He said it, He will bring it to pass. Weeping may endure for a night, but joy comes in the morning. Morning is coming sooner than you think, so just hold on to God's unchanging hand. And when you reach the end of your rope, just tie a knot and hold on—hold on. "For I know the thoughts that I think toward you, saith the Lord, thoughts of peace, and not of evil, to give you an expected end" (Jeremiah 29:11).

Warfare Prayer
(Pray before you start each day.)

Father in the name of Jesus, we first pray for those who have rule over us-all spiritual leaders and civic leaders everywhere. We bind all the works of the enemy and every satanic power and influence. We curse it at the root and satan we command you to drop your weapons and flee, for God has given us power and authority over all the works of the enemy. We are pulling down strongholds, principalities, powers and spiritual wickedness in high places. We come against police brutality, drive by shooting, rape, robbery, and mass murders. Satan we command you to cease and desist.

You have no authority, no dominion in our lives. Take your hands off of our children, our families, our homes our churches and our businesses in the name of Jesus. We bind all manner of sickness and disease. We command Covid-19 and all of it's variants to go into uninhabited places and leave this planet. We come against poverty and attacks of the enemy against our finances and in our homes.

We command you to lose our health and our wealth right now and take your hands off of God's people in the name of Jesus. We cast the devil out of the mind right now in the name of Jesus. Loose the mind, loose the will in the name of Jesus and we give you no place.

God has all power and all control and we have the keys to the Kingdom and we're walking in dominion power, kingdom power by the authority of the Holy Ghost. We are pulling down strongholds, casting out demonic spirits, trampling on spiritual wickedness in high places in the name of Jesus.

We command the blessings of the Lord to be upon us this day… the blessings of the Lord overtake us …the blessings of the Lord make us rich and add no sorrow in the name of Jesus. We are walking in victory; we are walking in authority; we are walking in power because greater is he that is in us than he that is in the world. No weapon formed against us shall prosper in the name of Jesus and thanks be unto God who has already given us the victory and causes us to triumph over every work of the enemy. We are walking in kingdom power and authority right now and we're seated in heavenly places in the name of Jesus.

We thank you for the victory. Victory in our homes, victory in our bodies, victory over our finances, victory in every area of our life.

Thank you Jesus for hearing and answering our pray.

Family Photo Gallery

Lady Shirley Wooten

Bishop Lawrence M. Wooten–Husband

Mother Hattie Adkins (Mother)
9/22/26 – 2/4/21
Mr. Hugh Adkins (Father)
8/22/25 – 10/3/91

Left to right (sisters & husbands) Mr. & Mrs. Herman Carter,
Mr. & Mrs. Carl Faison, Mother Hattie Adkins,
Mr. & Mrs. Roger Smith, Mr. & Mrs. Lawrence Wooten, Sr.

Grace S. Wooten
(daughter)

Sarah M. Wooten
(daughter)

Kimberly Wooten
(daughter)

Lawrence Wooten, Jr.
(Son)

Shelene B. McClendon
(daughter)

Mr. & Mrs. Jay James
(Son & wife)

Biography

International Evangelist Shirley A. Wooten is the First Lady of the Eastern Missouri Western Illinois, Jurisdiction COGIC and First Lady of Williams Temple, where her husband, Bishop Lawrence M. Wooten is the Prelate and Pastor, and Second Assistant Presiding Bishop COGIC.

Shirley Adkins was born in Boykins, Virginia, the second of four daughters born to Mr. and Mrs. Hugh Adkins. She received her BS degree (English) from Virginia State University in 1972. Additionally, while attending Syracuse (New York) University, she worked toward a Master's Degree in Public Relations Communication. She also received an honorary Doctorate Degree in Divinity from Malachi Bible College, and Doctorate of Humanities from Sacramento Theological Seminary and Bible College.

Lady Wooten began her career as a Sales Training Specialist with Carrier Air Conditioning Company in Syracuse, NY. She was the first African-American female to hold that position with Carrier. As a result of her outstanding career achievements, she was featured in Ebony magazine and Black Enterprise magazine. Later she became a Writer Producer for Maritz Corporation in Montvale, NJ. In 1978, she relocated to St. Louis Missouri to work for Southwestern Bell Telephone (currently) AT&T,

where she was Certified as a Course Developer, Public Speaker, Instructor and Internal Auditor.

Having mistakenly come to Williams Temple COGIC one Sunday morning and being unfamiliar with sanctification, she was saved, sanctified and baptized with the Holy Ghost in February 1979. It soon became apparent the true reason for her relocation to St. Louis. Evangelist Wooten is a dedicated Saint.

She lived a life of prayer and fasting and witnessing. In 1986, she became a licensed Evangelist Missionary and began to run revivals, in which many souls were saved and filled with the Holy Ghost. She has authored several booklets and literature on Faith, Fasting, and other topics relating to Spiritual Growth. She is well known as a Prayer Warrior, God Chaser and one who delights in putting satan on the run.

Working as her husband's help "meet", Evangelist Wooten serves/has served in the following positions:

- Director of Loving Care Adult Day Care
- Director of the Neighborhood Outreach and LMW Learning Center
- Coordinator of consecrations, fasts, shut-ins and prayer services
- Established and maintained daily prayer services, (6 AM to 4 PM) for three consecutive years where many were saved and delivered
- Public Relations Director for Eastern Missouri/Eastern Illinois Jurisdiction
- Co-President of Pastor's and Ministers' Wives Circle
- At the National level, Evangelist Wooten has served the COGIC, International in the following areas:

- ❖ Speaker at the National Revival Fire Service in Memphis
- ❖ Taught seminar at the COGIC National Leadership Conference
- ❖ Keynote speaker at the International Women's Convention/Crusade, 2010
- ❖ Co-Marshall International Department of Women
- ❖ At the International level, she has ministered several places:
  - ❖ U.S Virgin Island & Trinidad/Tobago
  - ❖ Uganda East Africa, where she not only ran a several week soul-saving crusade, but along with her Husband support many orphans, and also adopted a village to support. As a result of her Ugandan ministry, she and Bishop Wooten decided to add to their family of four children, by adopting their two youngest daughters from Uganda (Sarah & Grace).

Bibliography

- US Center for Disease Control
- Created For Commitment, by A. Wetherell Johnson
- King James Bible
- New York Times

CPSIA information can be obtained
at www.ICGtesting.com
Printed in the USA
JSHW052330300123
36928JS00006B/21

9 781662 856358